"The force that drives   s
Drives my red blood; ll   reams
Turns mine to wax.
And I am dumb to mouth unto my veins
How at the mountain spring the same mouth sucks

OFFSHORE

ANNE ATIK

OFFSHORE

London
ENITHARMON PRESS
1991

First published in 1992
by the Enitharmon Press
36 St George's Avenue
London N7 0HD

Distributed in the UK and Ireland
by Password (Books) Ltd.
23 New Mount Street
Manchester M4 4DE

Distributed in the USA
by Dufour Editions Inc.
PO Box 449, Chester Springs
Pennsylvania 19425

ISBN 1 870612 02 7

The photoportrait of Anne Atik
is reproduced by kind permission of Henri Cartier-Bresson.

The text of *Offshore* is set in 12pt Bembo by
Gloucester Typesetting Services, Stonehouse, Gloucestershire,
and printed by
Billing and Sons Limited, Worcester

ACKNOWLEDGEMENTS

The author and the Enitharmon Press express their thanks to the editors
and publishers of the following: *Poetry Chicago*, *The Nation*, *London Jewish
Quarterly*; and to Victoria Miro, with Simon Cutts of Coracle Press.

Front cover: Claude Gellée: detail from *Ulysses Restoring Chryseis to her
Father* (1647; The Louvre, Paris).

Offshore is also published in a large format de luxe limited edition of
85 copies (ISBN 1 870612 07 8), each containing two signed original
lithographs by Avigdor Arikha and R. B. Kitaj, and a photoportrait of
Anne Atik by Henri Cartier-Bresson.

Contents

MODELS AND THEIR PAINTERS

The Model and Her Painter

He wants too much. A bit of flesh, he says,
like unwitting Shylock. More in earnest.
Years he studied anatomy.
Now to flesh the bones on canvas.
Two or three strokes to express a knee.
The hip's crest traced, the elbow picked, with keys
of brown and red he's learned from masters,
who also taught that how he sees
affects the nature of the knee he shows.
If he wants motion not to move,
the instant trapped in full repose,
why does he require nudity?
Why doesn't he get himself a pepper,
leek, or tangerine, or rose?

And then we're not alone.
My ancestors crowd round me, looking on
while the nose and chin they gave me surface,
as though I were their epitaph.
True, he's kinder than Goya to some models'
weak mouths and warts.
More tact, like Bonnard's to his aging wife
(years I eavesdropped on art history).
He kept her youthful lines: a gentleman.
This one standing here may yet get mine
like Titian or Velázquez, if I'm lucky –
and if I'm not, like Bouguereau, or worse –
their nude was more than just a naked human.

9

But why exhibit all the parts
that 'nature placed more modestly away'
(Lucretius, urging measure in display)?
A dermis to the stranger,
the voyeur in the viewer.
What right has he to look upon my planes
and hollows, with whom I'd never talk
about my tastes, or dreams, or terror?
Though if I were shaped like Venus,
I wonder, to be honest, if I'd care
as much that all of me lies so exposed.
Except my presence.

THE SITTING, CONTINUED

Skin, he paints. The same way, after all,
that mystics glossed the Song of Songs as holy;
held human love as step to the divine,
naked flesh itself the parable.

Does this, then, make me just his vehicle?
My limbs, to him, a dare
of lines that flow across, athwart,
four winds, around, a motion?
If it were otherwise, I'd know.
I'd know the difference between appetite
and the undertaking as repast.
His greed for color, angle, stroke,
feeds him and me,
a viewer, at the last.

THE SITTING, DONE

It's a different species of skin.
Even though a likeness glows
in the copy he sees as good,
and the ochre and flake-white tones
get as close to the live as he can,
the original looks less labored.

One more thing I mean to protest.
What the painter can't avoid:
the left-out in what he tells.
What I was the hours I stood.
Like painting a pomegranate
and not the seeds with which it fills.

The real trades with such inward things;
blue leaving his moving brush,
or the bird-form that leaves my brain
suddenly glimpsed on an outward twig;
or an imperious need for sky
met with the sound of an airplane's drone.

And if, curbed, to gain altitude,
one can only spread inner wings,
only lift eyes, for height,
where's their trace, in what nature shows
when in her uncovering mood,
or what art can, when they close?

Against Rembrandt

I see them in all the great cities,
a patina on their golden frames,
the sitters in Amsterdam's sunset, shown
at an hour wound by the hand
of a painter growing old.

You can recognize them at once.
Not by their rank or repute, those
enclosed in archives and files.
But by what they invariably wear:
earth colors for earth's processes

from first dust unto last.
My sole reproach to the master.
There's no legacy there to others.
No lesson of touch or tone.
No matter how rich the turban, lavish

the lace, the pigments rush to the core
of one event, mainly – the certain
evidence of what's human:
the advent of a face.
What lesson is there to learn

about the decomposing heart in pain?
There, under our eyes, the bite
of sorrow, doubt, of those who looked
and knew, their eyes of charcoal burnt
with what they knew, even as they sat.

There's no craft to fire, once lit.
It glows, sputters, dies.
No technique to their swept lives,
those men and women in simple blows
of earth, fire, dust,

and no attempt at an answer
to what Leonardo, before a skull,
asked its ash-white socketed bones,
Dimmi. Tell me. Tell –
Just these gourd-gold, earth-brown tones.

Als Ich Can 17 June 1439

(*for Béatrice*)

MARGARITA

I, Margarita, am wife to one man twice.
Once to him my body and its being
are promised in wedlock; crown to toes
the boundaries of my soul that wears his ring.
And once to him who disembodies me
stroke by stroke, uncovered to the world,
then gaze by gaze by it again embodied.

With an oil tempera mix he rounds my cheek
once rounding out my father's filling palm,
and now reveals one ear as I sit listening
to the sound of sable brushing substance on.
The maid spills slush, the cook clangs iron pots;
dogs bark, my children call and scatter.
I'm in the painter's eye, but wholly other.

VIEWER

Did he tell you, Margarita, as you sat,
and he continued round your eyes, 'Matchless eyes!'
and then step back, appraising what he'd done –
the green cutting the carmine robe you wore,
the miniver and unbecoming coif?
Who else saw you that way – the courtier, butcher,
baker? Not for your beauty drawn from life –
als ich can, he signed,
though you don't look very beautiful –
they locked your portrait up in chains
when painters tried to steal it St Luke's Day,
but for the newness of his jeweled tones
and craft of generations in his hands.
Was that enough for you, did you want more?
Did his soul wear your ring, didn't you care?

MARGARITA

Care about exposure? Should I mind
that he painted all the wrinkles on my neck?
And made my lips too thin, too crabbed, a sign
of pique, economy or caution? Let us say
there are other ways I could have spent my time.
But he painted more and less than you can see.
This painted cloth holds only part of me.

VIEWER

What were you thinking when you let him sign
'*My husband Jehan finished me*'? So humble,
your thoughts packed off to a corner in your mind
like landscapes pushed to corners in the portraits
your countrymen so favored. You left no deed.
You might have taken up embroidery.
There you sit, indentured with your dowry.
Was it for posterity? The likes of me?
You may have known I'd look at you
looking at him, but it is he
who saves you from oblivion.
He might have failed, you might have never been.

MARGARITA

I'd have refused if color was less true.
The gift I sat to was a gift not his
to order from a muse on distant hills,
but one to serve, and from an inner height,
as well. I, too, feel chilled, am also stirred
when he paints light on light with thickened light.
Though my marrow's gelled, my needs shored up,
I'm not alone in heeding someone's will,
my face in one position, muscles bent.
He also is become an instrument,

and paints for his rapt, delighting, grasping eye.
Can you look with that upon me, viewer?
For if you'd rather probe what my life meant –
this painted cloth holds only part of me.
Watching him become an instrument,
I'm in the painter's eye but wholly other.

Note: *Als Ich Can* are the words inscribed by Jan van Eyck on the frame of the portrait of his wife Margarita.

At the Wallace Collection

Titus AND *Lady With a Fan*

They never met, except in that long room,
these intimates of a painter's hearth,
but now they're hanging face to face,
like strangers on a bus,
staring at a point my shoulders screen,
glancing each other's binding frames,
where no wary guard can intervene.

There's a wick in both of them the painters caught
with clearly more than paint for medium.
So similar it makes the strangers kin,
though ten years and a thousand miles apart.
So warm, the spine's alarms are sounded,
as it ushers a living presence in,
drawing the eyes like vessels on a rhumb-line
to that end of the room
as though someone had shouted.

She: 'the lady of singular perfection',
a diapason Velázquez played
in major ivory, minor white;
even if not his wife or daughter, shines
in a razor-slit's worth of light at her breasts
grazed with lace trim and reticence.
What is it radiates from those planes
that breaks down frail, though armed, defences?
What is it glows in the fan, the gleam
of bronze, like another 'Byzantium'?

He: Rembrandt's son in red beret,
golden chains and yellow-brown mantle;
a flame sputtering on the facing wall
one turns to with the cough and stir
that ease the weight of an andante.
Titus peers at something moving
only his father's brushes hold
in pigments alchemists may have dreamed
could be annealed to ounceless gold.

One day a curator will change their place:
will hang a nymph or cloud across the wall;
put them back in their period or school.

It will have been a pure coincidence:
the three of us, by different frames divided,
they, by a closing time
and familiar's touch, united.

YOUNG AND OLD

Touch Wood, Throw Salt

I gave the first one four names, four:
one for grace, one against illness, two for beauty.
I call her Bea, Aurora, call, Claire and Arabella.
Two against spite and the evil eye, two for beauty.

But then I grew more subtle,
and simplified precautions.

So gave the second two names, two:
one for strength in shadow, one, and one for beauty.
When she's sad, Zohara, call (or Hesperus), and Lucia.
One for light in dangerous places, one for beauty.

With guile – out of Ramah Rachel's voice
and molten weeping warn me –
With guile – out of Phrygia Niobe
in frozen grief reminds me –
And stealth – Demeter may stalk the fields
and David cry for Absalom
and fire, flood or accident
may befall, betide me –
I call four angels to their side,
those of Voyages and Ways:
Michael to the right of them,
Gabriel to their left,
Oriel ahead, Raphael behind,
and His Spirit above them.

Nothing alone has no names, none.
The two I've borne bear names and bone.
Lest they despair, lest they presume,
Aurora for dawn, Zohara for moon.
For morning, one, for evening, one,
and all for their living beauty.

Teaching Noga the Hebrew Alphabet

Her wide eyes move, fix.
Her small lips venture.
She's at the letter *kaf*, then *khaf*
and final *khaf*, like hope,
eleventh of a sacred script.
Looks up to see if it's correct, and smiles.
She says the letter twists like comet tails.
Her nine-year old tongue English-molded
in names for dolls, her bed, a dove,
glides into the fitting angle.
Her red mouth bites into consonants
in *kabed*, the root for Honor
thy father and thy mother. God knows
the remorse they bite me with for mine,
as for her faith in our unerring power.

From *khaf* she steps to *lamed*.
Chanting it, her cheek rounds out
like the mini-globe beside her.
Twelve past the aleph and the beth
whose curves settled in the void;
past the beginning to a world
accustomed to as being there before her.
She now has less than half to go
before she reads a simple Hebrew line.
The words for apple, garden, waters, dove.
Before she reads of heaven and earth,
of the spirit that hovers.

No gong resounds, and yet,
though I've uttered no warning,
'Child, look where you're going';
given no sign, and yet
she stops, dips, goes on with careful tread.
As though initiated.
As though aware that at the end
the primal words await her: *Ani*
Thou shalt   Thou shalt not

Kindling

The cry drifts from the wilderness. The child's.
And blow of a ram's horn. Innocence
Meant for me to hear.
                          I heard.
Meant to bend my doubts into obedience.
Doubts whose spreading tar sticks to my heels.
Doubt-knots in the ties that bid me listen
To the child's cry. Kindling,
Meant for penitence.

From far, a smell of flesh, over the woods,
Drifts, from afar, and settles where I am.
A burning thing, more flammable than doubt.
A scapegoat, ram, a heap the knife made numb.
Whose is that cry, that bleat of agony,
                          my father, my only one?
From where, that sound
That came in time – too late for Abraham,

So late for me, for us, whom you once dandled?
Our space usurped by a more distant one
For Whom you let us wait on a small bench,
Restrained by awe, outside your altered heart.
For Whom you shunned appeal until you'd done
With offering, although you left
                          the door ajar.

The cry was meant for me to hear.
                          I heard –
Your hand on my head trembled –
The horn, the father's call, the silent son.

Snapshot

Image of the coast in the two of us on the street.
You wading in the sea, I watching from the sand.

Or – like the coast holding back the sea, I hold you back
or hold you closer, depending on the danger.
You're waving your hand.
Mother and daughter, sea and surf.
As close where they part as where they meet.
I've been spinning the cocoon of my regret:
my weakness stamped on your agitation
like water on algae.
It's been six months since you left the house, a child
running frantic into womanhood.
There are many hours in the day I don't think of you,
but there are many hours in the day.

Obligations:
From the West to the East

I write to the old address again
and stop. Nearly forgot: block A or B?
Must check, like a too-familiar birth-mark.
Next, the area code of her empty nest
where I'd been born,
left, over depths of ocean,
for western mist; pack the words
on thin paper, to lighten their weight;
wings on the air-mail envelope
will home them eastwards. Under my pen
the steep street rises, the grey? shutters appear,
shrugging pinched shoulders. My mother's wave
from a square of the first-floor window
remembered now
makes my hand quiver, loosens its grasp on the pen,
ink-blots spread and billow.

Better to call her, over the Mediterranean.
Blue sea . . . nurse to numerous children,
to tribes and nations spawned near her waters
who kept her habits in cooler climates;
nurse to her who once nursed me,
her forgetful daughter.

I wait for her to cross the small room.
She takes so long – are the chairs in her way?
The phone's on the shelf, near my father's books
in the chest I remember; they row into view.
A voice that strains to sound nonchalant
answers in gulping waves through cables.
In her flowered? dress, her breath towards me
over the black receiver, now
as then, when contact was wireless.
The books row back as I mumble good-bye.

Finish writing as promised; street, section,
without stop or mistake. The facts as solid
as the gold ring on the thick wedding finger
of her trembling hand, that can barely grasp scissors,
that I can't hold or steady
as she opens this letter.

An Interruption

Had just read 'scourge', as, to beat,
when a burst of sleet rapped at the window glass,
grey light wringing its hands like an old mother.
Nineteen years ago, the same word noted
in another list, after a flash of ire, as, wrath
and need to punish.
Looked it up then for correct pronunciation
after some anger, but haven't uttered yet.

Strange comfort, stopping before a hail of nature,
the rap-tap sound. Sleet on a schoolday,
quelle misère! and they've left their gloves,
their briefcases sticky . . . They've come again,
these intruders on my quiet's landing;
how get them hence, as, out. They broke in
on another beat that was tapping, something
like the sound of sleet. Upon me
the same pall as nineteen years ago, moving
to the chest from behind the shoulders.
Was this what others felt, when a fog-horn lowed,
or a ram's horn, what the owl heard, foraging
for her young in stirred, rumoring feathers?
The pumping sound in the soul's sump,
cesspool, under the many-staircased house
of a poem: the light-footed iamb, lifted,
the trochee bowing low, the three-fingered dactyl
flashing neat wrists, the turnabout anapest,
anapest, foiled! – Such slim ankles
hold up the entire edifice,
the intruders on every landing
now locked in with the rest.

Variations on an Enigma

Shall I go when I am bidden,
or offer quinces to the gods, instead,
fed to satiation?
Placate them with crisp argument of apples?
The moon's in Asia, turning her other cheek
away from Helen's dust-filled eye,
far from once well-tended fields
bulldozers have stolen, even
those of Arcady.

Shall I go when I am bidden?
Leave my life in a parcel tied
with crimson, flowing ribbon
at a bustling supermarket, with some fruit
meant for my children? Down the dwindling
clumps of trees, road companions, felled,
already recede from the horizon.
The stream of stars and streaming rivers
prepare the earth for plowing, for
replacing spent roots rhythmically
with new ones, nourished till their time,
quietly accepting its direction.

        And I could wish such pliancy were mine.
The cries of those who couldn't wait their turn,
who couldn't bear their state alone
of rootedness, uprootedness,
whose hearts' ropes and pulleys frayed,
you hear in wails of an ambulance's siren,
loud echo of vague oracles
they've stopped propitiating.

But I must wait till bidden.
And though a worm devour
apples' fragrant arguments, their seeds
are planted in my children's core.
And though the moon, obedient,
celestial, navigating sphere,
will soon come back from Asia – it's not
sublunar passions that attract her;
she'll shine where Helen's bones lie forgotten,
and other beauties wash upon the shore –
I'm moved by different tides from hers
        that I could wish were shallower.

Dyeing Day

Woman to Dyer

The grey, cover the grey with balms and henna
before night comes. Cover the grey, the years.
Nature has told the truth. Cover the truth
before age streaks in, telling a lie.

What's the color of desire, what's its age?
That its gorge, swallowing, runs shallow with time,
then dries, the young never doubt. Ask those
who know its time: it goes down wells at sunset,
they'll tell you, deeper than at dawn.

Dyer to Woman

Grey weighs as much as rain.
The word weighs less than a hair.
With these vials and bottles I borrow
what poets borrow from nature
with the words: gold, raven, fair.

No resin, no turpentine
can rinse off the unprimed canvas the young
paint their youth upon,
from which age slowly emerges
with layers of care painted on.
With hands in an ancient gesture but
with untaught diligence
they powder on purity, blush, impatient
with innocence.
Madonna-blue shadow on lids brim
glances that foretell
an event that they hope only they
and gravid night will reveal.
Over their own guardian brows
they draw on, with eyebrow pencil
brows borrowed from memory;
two lines written once in praise
bestowed on another's eyes.

I use such ink for my dyes.

Woman to Girl

Poets are to blame for the paint that you've put
on your face turned into a metaphor.
Had they not compared hair to a field of wheat,
eyes to sloes, or boats by a shore;
breasts to twin roes – or grapes, if you will,
you'd not have stroked on beauty in rites
practiced in sunlight or bulb-light;
the beauty of the tribe.
And all for a tithe of their tribute.
Rouge and kohl a carnate homage to incarnate
poetry. The thigh joints like jewels
and ivory-towered neck as in Solomon's lines,
or the bloom of Burns' and Waller's rose –
these drive young girls in chagrin
to see if the mirror shows
just a neck, or an ivory tower;
just the lips, or the two red, ripe cherries
of Herrick and Campion,
just a cheek-bone, or Yeats' sucked-in wind.
The beloved a cluster of camphire.
First blame poetry's power. Then the listener
whose ear words ravish and prod.

Girl to Woman

Blame a seed for needing sun?
Someone visible wants to be seen.
Blame beholding, or the beholder.
The portent of a face
is that it faces an other.

Woman to Girl

One day, one night, one time, your face
unparabled, uncompared, will be lit
by the hearth behind your beloved's eyes,
like a cameo on a coat, love lending
the colors you've now colored there.
Oh, of course he'll swerve his lids and delight
when youth enters, smoldering in red and gold
and bangles, like a splendid fire-engine.
But he has a place to keep in order, its candle's
worth of shelter, bights of custom there.
Love holds a cordial mirror
to greying, thinning hair.

Girl

Your jealous eyes skim the mirror.
Your resigned hand-me-downs are a sham.
I've caught you, too, in the ritual,
smoothing your hair, your hem
before answering the doorbell.

Poor faces which we must wear
knowing that they are seen
as proof of what we are –
tenants of a pinch-lipped landlord
to whom high rent is due,
our skulls collateral,
not what they hide from view.
What were my dolls but bounds
of the dollmaker's imagination,
confined to smiles and pouts?
Though their glass eyes shed no tears,
foam hearts didn't give way –
for dolls are consolable
bits of rag and imperfection –
I learned how inches swayed

a timbre, a gesture, gait,
how often the dimpled smiled,
how others turned if they cared
that their nose was too wide or too long.
Vanity? Blame the beholder.
In books and poems only beauty
is toasted with a song.

Woman

For song's sake. Not the list, but the air's
sake. And for whose sake do you paint yourself
for battle – for a troubador and his roll-call
of past beauty? For a stage-prince, elegant
in boots and brilliantine, unsure of his part?
For your good text, get a good reader
who may cherish precious bindings, but
will get your lines by heart, for your own sake.
In the ancient tongue, for beauty,
but the vernacular, for love.

Girl

But tonight, tonight, I must go,
this very night, enter a room,
enter indifferent glances
in which seats someone has settled:
a peerless beauty. She
with lips like a thread of scarlet,
legs like pillars of marble.
If I'm not of silk and scarlet,
who'll choose the soul in me?
Should I carry the cochineal
and silkworm on my arm?

Woman

Bud lightly, we bid our daughters. But lightly.
That room you'll enter, you'll leave
heavier with a flower's fulness those
who plant flowers come to grieve.

Girl

But now the moon has got me, old women say.
Now I count, and can't account for my veins'
ebb and flow. Or if it's not the moon,
it's the rush of seasons merging.
Desire and seasons merging. All ordained, foreseen,
this rush, when you engendered me.
Kohl and powder in the plan for continuity.
What solace, the plan, when my ashes
will join those of a rose or onion
in a cycle of still more ashes?

Woman

It may be according to plan, a planner's insatiate wishes.
Or faceless voracity. But what woman bears with man
can make a poem of ashes, love another of song and ashes
before dwindling, according to plan. Between us and earth
there's poetry's hyphen. It won't leave our flesh alone
in its fragility, but compounds it with a flame
into more than flesh can be.

Dyer

But flesh goes grey with dust
for all the dyes I hold.
Grey weighs as much as rain
and lies with raven and gold.
Time puts last things last
the living put first again.

Adultery

Earnest friendly talk and then
eyes – do you really –
rather. And then eyes
do you, do I.
Turn the head away, friendly
talk, good night, avert
once more. Look; shake hands,
comic-strip electric bracelets
shock the wrists. Then eyes.
I do. Must not.
How in the street scarves tightened,
coats' collars raised. Chill.
Good night, taxi hailed.
Look. Fire. Who sees?
A fourth of a second. Who saw?
Shaken. You too.
Turn back; don't insist
on combustion. Charming smile
includes all. Coat hides
rounding breast. Impossible.
Good night. An old word like a sword
hangs between them. An old trust
like a trellis spreads, arrests them
from running into one another's skin.
She knows, she knows, it's his desire
sends currents of desire over her.
Beware of fire, avoid the wrists.
One person saw, with singed indifference.

After Ironing

She is neater than the censor in a dream.
She folds the clothes still warm from pressing,
lays them in piles in order of importance
with grave regard to gender.
They touch but do not mingle with each other.
The intimate and outer, sleeve to sleeve,
neck to waist, the frivolous and plain.
What tangled in the wash, batch of confusion,
she separates again.

To envy her would be unthankful.
Or ask that sleep or good advice
smooth out the ragged with such ease;
that one will wake, recovering
the sense of what will wear, which seam will stay
another onslaught
on what's frayed or gossamer,
on this tissue flung with grace around the bone;
or leave alone what irons only touch
at the risk of burning.
Or to stay impeccable, till the end . . .

Now to put them in their place.
A privilege of afterthought.
Arrange the starched, the flowing
apparel of appearances
according to their distance from the sun.
Spring and fall, dune and lawn
on different hangers.
Allowing for some turbulence –
shirts with lavender, picked wild, and scarves
with clove-pierced oranges exhaling groves –
chronology, the housekeeper, ticks on.
Moves steadily from shelf to shelf.
Here for day, there for night.
For the armed, the naked self.

But you . . .
            if only you . . .
Chaos in your chest.
Its contents in a jumble, visible.
As telling as the diary of a shell
that shows how neap – and high – and flood-tide beat.
A shambles, your heart's chambers.
No time-divider in its drawers.
Late and early loss, paired
like nearly matching socks, leave notched
lines above your brows.
If only you . . .
            So prodigal,
            wearing it all.
Potpourri of dream and waking.
Wearing it out.

The Next Time

(for Jocelyn Herbert)

I thought that it could wait till after dark.
Till after tea, till after they'd been done,
the duties I thought day
imposed on me.

So sure they'd hold, those faces in the bus.
That old man's, raked, scythed –
he'd been a man so long a time –
asking to sit down, hand to his hat,
pity sucked from people's seated eyes;
a seat was all age pleaded for.
That lithe girl's, stamped and sealed with youth
delivered to a young man at the stop,
smiles widening in rhythm
on both sides of the opening door.

It seemed that such a sight as had flashed by
of the aged about to part from flesh,
of the young running into vernal arms,
of passengers with magazines, believing
in advice and recipes torn out
to try out before long
but stacked away in overflowing drawers,
would keep until I'd write it, in some peace
I could not yet afford.

But I was wrong.

That moment and a thousand others passed
since yesterday; have fallen like the drops
of rain now wasted in the street
but urgent as a pulse in time of drought.
To think that I'd recall it,
what street it was, or the color eyes, the hat.
The perfect present that had come in time,
to think it'd be the same
when looked at late.

I've long since had my tea, my dark, my dawn.
I've done what I thought others asked of me,
though they had not expected all they got;
had not required once
this night my soul
that never will have peace it can afford,
though it wait, and wait.

My Father's Lesson

(for T. Carmi)

What I was asked to do when taught to pray
was, not to kneel,
but flicker like a candle.
Torso the blue
and shoulders the yellow flame.
The spine a lighted wick
of understanding.
With each approach to the Holy Name,
each blessing,
on fruit, fragrance, scholars, safety, storm,
my father swayed,
neared by a hail of feeling.
And I, in a slower current.
did the same.
Whoever calls, he said, must have sharp hearing,
should an answer come.
A low knock on the door
could as well be the Messiah as thug or neighbor.
So that, though guttered
white with weariness,
there was no day when dailiness
was slighted.
First he'd praise, and afterwards, feel thankful,
intone the Shema, the Hear O Israel,
tines that pronged me to
devotion.

That was in childhood, when delight in the day's
fruit and fragrance wells up unprompted.

I forget the reason I let my house swell with clutter
and shelves of reasons.
Though my hearing's sharp,
I'm not sure anyone's listening,
and won't call out,
though in an advancing season.
Listening, I hear the two sides of rustle.
The claims of water under the eaves, dropping.
The case roared by storm to those it ravaged, suit
I've had no choice in.
Not ready yet to plead for
flaws, the core of questions.
Not ready yet
to let my voice break
remembering the touch of those
who loved without asking
ransom of answers.
My spine, a stump of a wick; joints stiff
from a long-since sloughed position.
I try to call
on stir, on motion, to seize my shoulders.
Grope
for an all-proof match in a laser age
to strike me
to light me
so that I may
flicker like a candle.
Ask
to be able to ask, to sway,
at least on occasions.
Ready myself for prayer
by praying,
silent as ice that readies itself
for cracking.

Haute Couture

Then from Divine Cloth cut a bolt of skin
    as a child would a moon
    of papier mâché.
And with Divine Thread sewed the hems of a human –
    With a spider's patience.
    With a tailor's skill
    allowing for ease in arm or thigh.
    With a surgeon's care in patching what's torn
    by napalm, plague or passion.
Through Art Sublime sheathed the smallest cell,
gave the blood stream, tubes, orifice,
the immunity of Paradise.

Then in Divine Compassion cut out a mate
and – setting conditions – trees bearing fruit
    under which to delight, to lie,
    multiply, spar, accommodate.
Then brought in Death. Only then looked away.
    Discarded, they wrote about whence they had come,
    about the Designer, Cloth and Design.
He sat back from it all.
From the trapped spider and thrashing soul
    unable to swim.
From the stapled bodies hurled into spin.
With containment divine . . .

Checklist

Not cold, not hot – medium.
Not hungry. Moderately full.
Children all right – another story.
Husband facing it. Shirts ironed.
Vitamin pills. No lumps.
Shoes polished, in repair. Clothes back
from the sloppy cleaner's.
A friend's distress – some sympathy.
Mozart's Requiem from a facing window.
Not the right moment.
No elation. No despair.
All this in order – tolerable –
now how write a poem?
News from another window.
An earthquake in El Salvador.
Summit meeting in Iceland.
Another story.
Taxes paid. No outstanding debts.
Hair washed. Can go on all right.
A bit of dust, this morning's.
This moment, in a corner.
Slept enough. How write a poem?
Clear enough in last night's dream.
A face grimaced, teeth bared, clenched,
hissing 'This is a poem!'

Close the window.

Old age some – small – way ahead.
Doubts. Well-oiled.
How write a poem.
Light in my household.
Must get some candles.

In a Retirement Home

She's dreaming the unaged dreams
of the old. And the indignities
that pills have mercifully masked
of tremors, incontinence,
are stingless at her dreams' threshold.
Idle, an unconsulted library,
she drowses with her lavish, oral text
on keeping home with seemliness,
worn pages in her yellowed palms, closed.
Her body, like a crowded bookshelf, sags.

She'd been a poet of the hearth before,
of saffron strings, shallots in vermeil skins,
of golden asters put in pewter jugs
where, though she didn't know their names, they glowed.
Plastic banned, things sang of earthen ware,
glass, some china, a wooden table.
She'd practiced what are waived as women's tricks:
making liquids work on stone,
with broth for a hardened grudge, tea for aches;
or cooled the smart from an insult's gravel
with some made-up news, sometimes a bit of salmon.
She'd listened gravely to the very young,
resignedly to neighbors.
Then, worn out after miles of compassion,
would take some rest in silence, her mother tongue,
one she spoke without grammatical errors.

She's now in a wheel-chair, bewildered.
No one can comfort her for not conferring
comfort, her giving gift foiled
without her tools of kettle and porcelain cups.
A doze, a nod, a lingering
old woman, she's left to the dreams of the old,
from time to time moving her parchment lips.

Face to the window, blue-turbaned, paralyzed,
she waits for guests in a room with formica tables.
Deaf in one ear, she has to be tapped on the shoulder.
Her face, massed coral reefs, breaks into smiles
so momentous – no, not like the glimpse ahead
of a traveled-to suddenly looming mountain,
but the crumpled body so alight, rising like bread,
it seems divine, an earthly notion.

OFFSHORE

Aubade in Paris

This dawn is treacherous
as I lie listening to the steady rain
dripping loudly on the balcony.
It may be that I've been here too long
in another language not to hear
the sound of Verlaine's rain as song –
comme il pleut sur la ville.
A blue-toned hoot from the owl near-by
in the convent garden calls, one syllable
with no accent to identify.
I must tell you, though, how in sleep I miss
small, rain, down; being loved
in English, with clipped consonants
of musk, stub, breach; the strong
English shoulder against Latin cheek.
A shoulder I now wish were next to mine
to lean on, like a familiar window-sill
to the bird alighting peregrine.
I know, I know: a trust mispronounced
but kept, outweighs the glib
though idiomatic lies that chill.
Yet with your arms to listen to,
comme il pleut sur la ville
translates to another lover's call.

But stay, he might have said, in those days,
stay, keep a space between you and me,
for without its shield I shall lose all – hope,
                    he might have said,
a horn in the distance, in one lone call
echoing the owl's. Oh, that my heart burst
                    now in your flesh,
he would have said, in the garden,
dawn a red patch, a jongleur – snickering? –
in those days, flattening a rose.

Her cheeks graphed with mascara.
Muck on his boots. His glasses fogged.
Il pleure dans mon coeur.
The mirror mists over. One last glimpse
of the glinting habergeon.
She waited, once, for the death of the dragon
amid the medieval clangor, but waits
no longer. The knight is taken.
The jongleur now dismissed decides
to whistle behind rent tapestries for spite.
The watchman calls out morning. In its light
they end the manuscript. The owl's hoot fades
as I waken from another tongue
I've read but not heard spoken,
a dream's charades.

My hands carve signs in cuneiform,
from right to left; the stores I offer
your hands reach for from left to right;
it's just that my ears starve at the banquet
I myself prepare.
                    This, mon cher,
is how I have betrayed you through the night:
the rain I hear this break of day
slants in iambic English feet,
steps with its falling, rising feet
to music that enisles me here
and locks you out.

For the Left Hand

(to Eugene Istomin)

The right hand leads the way

I doubt, but follow.
Mine the hand under the neck,
the head upthrown.
I hold down the paper, or chin
in my palm, fare thee well.
I tremble on the knob.
I repeat, regret, remember.

First to the shoulder in an embrace.

It signs the big deal or farewell note.

It bangs the door in anger.
It protests, exclaims, exhorts.
It carries the burden on the conductor's left,
but stalks center stage.

Then echoes the burden.
All cello, I. Grave, low.
Warn of more to come.
foes lunge from the left.
Where the erl-King thrums.

Rising violin-high, asks how it happened.

When the Lord's on the right
Whipped waves threaten. Flood over.
It stabs the tenor, the traitor in bed,
in the final aria, in the name of love,
Violin-high, why did it happen.

in the losing of.
All cello, I.
Can't weep for falling.
Sink darkling, dun.

It points the bunched fist to the heart on the
right

that breaks on the left.

We're rarely together.
We fold in a lap, contort, clap,
curve to bring a face closer.

Song can do without me.
But I support the theme.

A bird has no accompanist.
Its song rises lightling.

From harmony to harmony.

48

In Schubert, in Verdi,
death comes through its knuckles.
Struts in saccades.   It soaks clothes in water the quicker to drown.
I tamp stray hairs down.   It turns the crank for the organ-grinder,
                                                       that Leiermann.

Mine the groan, mine the sigh
of the Leiermann.
                    A stone has neither right nor left.
                    A word has neither left nor right.
Roundness needs my form.
                    Two hands across a freighted chest
                    take up less room.

Hideout

An experienced refugee, the soul.
Mans its own power station, antenna
camouflaged with lids and nails, listening
to tones no spy can overhear, that issue
lower than the lowest plaint can utter,
higher than hope's ultrasonic pitch.
Crouched in a cleft heart, ambush-wary,
its passport clutched, when raided, in its eyes.

Jumps out of bed, withdraws itself yet farther,
terror covering its mouth, with small belongings:
a lark at dawn, a *lied* that made it shudder;
the question children asked with satin cheeks
for which sake parents shattered rocks to answer;
the large space after crumbs were cleared, the slice
of laughter; a poet's line passed with dessert.
That soul pants as it tries to hide the cache

like a hart before the slaughter. Hide that heart
where there's no room for hiding. There's another
that it hails: Man ahoy, ahey, a man
like him alone, a one, in shoals, down under,
flight brings near to Sheol, runs on.
No refugee has ever failed to see
the requitedness of running, though the rest
may only teach him unrequitedness.

Run, then, run, and see how far it gets you.
There may be respite till the next attack.
Run till you're downed by power failure,
by fear, or fire, or even flight.
In any case your treasure's useless
to the secret agent at your back.

True North

By its light tea-traders peer, rejecting the débris
for the better leaves of Assam, Oolong, Yunnan.
In its light
lapis cuff-links turn to midnight blue;
a change not of stone, but of meridian.

> While from the south
> the light is good for plants and fruit
> and amorousness, though not the measuring eye.

It's by north
painters make out tones less mutable,
cold and warm least red with flattery.

> East – good for sculptors and architects
> and, ever east, for pilgrimage, for those
> who seek the most God-easterly point of all.

Straight by north,
should radar instruments give out,
helmsmen steer away from verging shoals.

> West – for the wind on which some poets call.

But only by north
I gauge the damage of a second's course.

> I am a merchant of the self,
> selling off false merchandise.
> Pass off what's lit by east or west
> as though they had a greater worth
> and keep to myself what's best.

Deception

How gladly I run when I most long to stay.
Hang on to assent as to a swooping cliff.
Remain in the sun when I most long for shade.
Like a fox playing dead when longing most for life.

Traveling Lightly

Looked through dictionaries and gold-
dusted thesauri.
One word under another
far from its birthplace,
exile at the cradle.
But with those words at my command
I must continue as is.
As is.
And I must confess:
few words at my command.

I sleep late in other poets' gardens,
in Babylon and Arden;
smell their woodbine, lie by their willows.
Sloth looses worms in my entrails
from apple-fallen Eden.
My camel's head turns towards distance.
Solitude hangs like a tongue in my mouth.
I have come this far.
Thus far.
My promises a burden

to keep to the silken route of skin
time hatches with noughts and crosses
until it cancels the row.
To map more lists for tomorrow,
word under word,
specks in a caravan,
with but a few of love at my command.
And I must confess:
the ones I have, a burden,
as is.

Landing Card

(after Tiananmen Square)

Where I am:
at the second point after etc..
On a one-way road to the third

                    that leads

to an empty, vast, final Sahara
white as the roots of hellebore

                    middle-age breeds.

What my state:
between liquid and solid: glass.
Suffused with breath that clouds over,

                    or flakes

with peering then vanishing faces
that leave no trace of their grimace or smile when

                    the surface breaks.

Of their cherished faces.

What I have to declare:
what shall I declare –
perfume and sherry – or failure

                    to act

in the charged, compelling air;
when asked what I've done can I say more than that
I saw the condemned being dragged on the screen

                    and just sat?

List what, in this common market
of sapient self-delusion?
Some checks, protests sent; a word
to a desperate friend; or the jade
and rubies past seasons lined in the mind's
false-bottomed bags – I swear,

                    other than that,

and a hollowness at the core,
I have nothing to declare.

Member of the Audience

It's when the fingers can hold back no more.
When the last note stops reverberating
and the pianist must get up, must show it's over,
what happened in that short half-hour.
It's then, the chord and note held back no more –
The applause. The relief at letting go.
Oh, eloquent and dumb, they clap,
and mute, for whom the pianist's fingers spoke.
Unclasp their hands, and pound them, now it's over.
One hand against the other;
the ear a silent devotee.

Moved, against all reason, nearly to tears
by their applause,
almost as much as by the music,
I sit among them, as mute and dumb as they.
Equally applauding with the others,
make the heady sound of praise, the heart's assent
the deaf composer couldn't hear
and may or may not have been waiting for.
Beat my hands, become an audience
with the hundreds row on row,
their eyes satin with gratitude.
Sitting in their dress of chest and spine
exposed in A flat major. In depths
they hadn't known they felt in just such notes.
Perhaps were never felt until composed.
Resumed in that half-hour.

It must have happened to them this way.
Or it's their own feelings they applaud.
Or both at once may be the case.
But with the last note in my head, the chord
held and there reverberating,
I know consensus can go just so far.
That only I have heard it thus.

Summer Vignette

Our neighbors' shutters are closed.
The windows they looked through squint –
blank in a high-rise crossword puzzle.
We water their plants on our terrace
cluttered with dropped intentions
stacked in trunks. Rust has undermined
the locks with the passing of seasons,

with ambitions we've left at the dry-cleaner's
to be picked up for better occasions
or abandoned, for still better reasons,
to others less resigned.
And it mattered, but mattered greatly, though
the occasion passed, the body still present,
that appearance match with the time,
the silk with garden or tweed with heather,
before they were put back on hangers.

Window-dressers unpin their promise
of triumph and right demeanor
from arch-lipped plastic dummies.

Some water has spilled down below,
cooling the sticky concrete
where workers, preparing for winter's
galoshes, have rolled up a street
Hermes cunningly crosses in sneakers.

A man above us, a sailor once,
tackles solids with a hammer,
things come undone, yet to be.
He remembers the names of some harbors,
his sighs blowing trade; talks of berries,
veers to restaurants, prices, wrenches,
his plain thoughts in their pyjamas.

The toy car in his son's small hands
holds an idea of greater motion;
a miniature of hope – that expanding
gas supplied to all apartments
with its onion smell – that evanesces
with the heliotrope and magnolia.

What hours flowers keep
before they're braced in vases:
the althaea, 10–4,
like our public library,
closed to courtship after.
Not like your evening primrose
who works later, leaning nightward,
like the wooing passion-flowers.

This was learned, not in fields or woodland,
but in pages leafed through with longing.

As was distance, the remote vista opened
by history's travel agents,
listing places time spent men in:
Hastings, Constantinople,
Magdeburg, Goa, Gomorrah
and the mystery of Cremona.
What star shone on Cremona?
Whose visit made it gravid
with violins of Amati,
Stradivari or Guarneri?
Their shops have closed for their night.
But their fingers are inseverably wound
with the music-latent wood
shaped with dents, like ears, for sound
that shaped hearing.
The girl next door plays Prokofiev's
presto while her Romeo leaps
from her balcony to surer ground.

Quassia amara of Surinam:
the bitter root, perfumed with vowels,
is the druggist's tonic for craving,
for departure, for Venice's light.

How else can the city's summer-breath hold out
against the dreams of far, fragrant gardens,
with beauty sleeping in Fahrenheit?
For it matters, it matters greatly,
where, without us, it spends the night.

Sonnets to Terry Who Died Young

This page upon your death you would have hated,
beauty sleeping in the silent wood, lying
with the trees' arms round your stung, receding arms,
leaves drifting, the chill swans dying;
you'd have abhorred your life-flight caught in rhyme,
who found the grammar of our being faulty
though no clause broke your loyalty's straight line,
no full stop once resumed your final beauty,
sleeping beauty in the fell, brooding wood
whom no Prince's probing kiss can waken;
struggle greyed only two strands in your hair
when death sat by, the patient, hooded falcon
loose in the hospital, his talons poised.
The poems you loved you read between his claws.

It's not for you I write, but for my pain
round which, a sharp, suspicious dog, I turn
first sniffing at the apple compote and then
looking up a synonym for mourn,
an eczema of pain, a spreading rash
of slugs and ash. For that and not for you
this page – and what is it to you, my friend;
your hazel eyes anxieties that saw
and looked away with swan indifference
at the river through blurring panes, wending;
my heart a fort of plastic, my hand a fraud
attempts to write of your flight and beauty ending.
You'd have despised it, the future it strips you of,
but done the same for that death you'll never live.

My memory tastes of medlars and persimmons,
best sampled when they rot, in a spilling pantry,
preserves in jars of all that now is not
(I, too, shall sprout brown fruit for autumn's bounty
and nature's thrift); of how you woke to ether
from dreams of heaths, poems as far from your bed
as a giraffe from its heart, making itself
invisible in the mimosas overhead;
from dreams of hawthorns and autumn's last words
in the reeling wild ducks' cries that led the hunter
to your caged-in breast, your waking, ambushed eyes;
of how you left, your gloves and dreams behind,
of how they fade if they're not stored in lines.
They die, the dead, if they're not borne in mind.

Writing Materials

Begin with the silver pencil you gave me
for writing poems; its thin, black lead;
your old drawing-pad with creamy paper; sunny room
a good friend lent me, a Webster's on the shelf;
go on to the new typewriter erasing thoughts
without a trace or doubt the old one showed.
Had lunch before I left so as not to stop,
though brought a navel orange, just in case . . .
There's heating, but my fingers are still stiff
in this February cold.

All this –   for what –
for the empty white.
Yours, white canvas before which you despair.
Mine, the ream of paper on the right side of the desk.
I've had no reason yet to reach so far.

I look through the drawing pad and find a child's scribble
in orange crayon, made once on a train,
in restlessness, in infancy.
I had lent her a page from what was meant for poems
and looked through the window's transparent pane,
the trees, rails, infant's scrawl unregistered.
There's also a list of honey-birds
drawn up, in the event –
that, and her orange scribble of four years ago
is all the drawing pad contains.

With this viaticum,
so fervently given
in hope that an event, even little –
with these elegant provisions, pressure-markers
of what-being-who rings in the head,
of that internal heat that sets off fission,
I'm waiting, prepared, and writing this instead.
If I could give you lines, a bare return,
some words that could stand up to glacial white,
that you'd remember, maybe, someday on a train,
I should have earned, if not my day
or minute's worth, enough for a short prayer,
at least your pad and pencil; say,
the page that this is written on.

Two Sonnets to Sight

I

I used to think that harmony was two.
I loved the beauty of an even number
in wrists, brows, wings or doubled yew,
until a virus, dressed in darkness' armor

rushed in and slyly curtained half my view.
With my Cyclopean eye that dared not close
I broke the habit nature bred in me
and learned what every poet blindly knows:

Two is the counterfeiter, symmetry,
pasting number and sidedness to things,
shrinking horizons still wide in me.

Halved but whole, and overcome with sight,
I didn't dare believe the half I saw:
one held as much as two of dark in light.

II

I was wakened by a song of thanks for fracture.
A scrap from Psalms, come like a guest, sat down
within my chest, chanting till dawn drew near
praise in Hebrew rhyme for the more-than-none.

My hours slowly closed a sundial's stare.
I saw no less in blur than profile hides,
the other side divined as breathing there;
the half-screened lips on which whole presence lies;

the splintered ray that filled with caulking sun;
the sum of broken things, of parts of one.
I recognized that song of the degrees:

David's, plucking harmonies as bidden,
but raising, to the hills where he thought hidden
help awaited, dimming, searching eyes.

The Nero Syndrome:

(to Nehama)

qualis artifex pereo

The dog in me will not bite.
The muzzle I feel on my mouth, through spite
for underachieving
keeps back thoughts from spilling
like the rave of canine saliva.
But I'm tamed. There's really no danger.
Myself is the nearest ear, yet
I crave now another.

The mind's clipped wires and cords are
my trophies for acts of failure.
I resisted the charge of the Muses
shot in buses, at the post office.
Preferred a mute quietus,
settling deeper under a blanket;
lulled an opus to sleep, to appease
a crouched brute.

It's a common disease I carry, for
you catch it from skin exposure.
To quash it I mimic repose.
Become my own anti-body:
mimic conscience and wakefulness.
In my fingertips traces of those,
as in needletips of pine trees
there are traces of buried gold
over which they chance to be planted.
Sometimes I shake off my spleen's
grip, haunted

by Nero as beast; a snarled sound
replacing the music he'd smothered,
a monster unleashed in his blood.
Knowing even then, what's interred
with the death of a man, what pages
of unrendered beauty the grave
closes upon
as he set Rome to ashes
and the rubble we're standing on.

A Little Member

How will you die?
By your tongue you shall die.
Not of sickness or age.
By your querulous, toadying, flailing tongue,
that hedge that lies
between inner rage and the teeth's closed gate.
By its scimitar
whose blade of blame and arrogance
splits friendships' hive, spilling the honey
laboured at.

Thus will you die.

Treacherous tongue.
Thought's gauche companion;
mangling its seeds with fat weeds of words
till thought falls by
like grain rain slowly cultivates,
but grows – in intent.
Blurting, unfaithful,
begging for crumbs at opinion's gate,
for a morsel of notice and smiles
quickly spent.

Remorseful, die.

By declaring your love,
love put on its hat and went.
By hissing out hatred,
hate settled down to squat.
By offering comfort,
grief deepened, reticent.
How then take back
the words sent out too late, too soon,
through the mouth's slotted door –
and what sounds make
to utter what a moment meant
that has run by,
but speak no more,

and, speechless, die?

The Cloth

It's scalpel-cut, then stitched together,
the dermic cloth that's on the bone
that years have spun.
There's a hole disease and age's
worm began.
You wear them both, the prey and predator.

You can make out the design, but not the meaning
of material as close-fitting as a rind,
when you are born,
but ravelled in the ground.
A design combining cloth and worm
that if asked, perhaps, you'd not have chosen.

Like the surgeon stapling clamps
and pins into yielding skin,
you staple what coherence
you can take cover in.

Inheritance Tax

I've nearly repaid all my debts.
The unconveyable
is all of my fortune that's left.

Each year adds more to those holdings
I can't bequeath.
And yet reduces their interest,
debases their worth.

In what coin can I reimburse
the capital lent at my birth:
all that called me to attention?
Not with those in my purse, or with words
for gifts others bestowed, and I spent,
of wit as unreckoned as salt,
and spice-boxed warmth or desire,
of their quirks, their passionate faith
in written lines, color or chord;
what in childhood seemed showered by God,
lift of day, spread of noon, fall of night;

or the gnawing side of the ledger:
the carry-a-one of injustice
my elders left me to correct
that I left ignored on the slate.
The accusations and slights
on stairs or public places,
or the waiting side of a desk.
Inadequate replies.
Adequate replies.
The regret at being wrong
still greater at being right.

Those portions devalued since,
I marvel that any of it's mine.
But whose, this munificence,
and miser's hoard of old wounds,
whose, when I've gone?

Civil Wedding

Get up at dawn to make the train.
Squash resentment – why at 11:30 sharp? –
at dressing up. Feel foolish.
The other passengers in workday clothes
and purpose, reading, yawning.
Three hours' ride, and it's raining.

A good dozen of us get out at Dijon.
Begin the trudge to the Town Hall.
Suddenly, seeing our number
opening umbrellas, our role unfurls:
we're now a congregation.
The ceremony is begun
by our merely attending, summoned
to hear that a man and woman mean
what they mean together – old words
of honor, love, protect. An old faith
pinning fresh flowers in pressed buttonholes.
A promise made between themselves,

but we, the procession,
we, the bells.

Incognito

(for Helit)

It carries chocolate to her armchair,
tells jokes, an apophthegm,
chats, admires the flower arrangements.
Gives some addresses, gets up to leave,
the pleasures of friendship mutually agreed on.
But in that last minute, as he comes in,
seduces.

Traitor. What have I to do with you?
I bring you to old friends, repay their kindness.
I dress you discreetly, trust your senses.
How come you shot off your big, fat cannon-
ball aimed at pleasing? Flirt, make advances,
dilate the pupils, lashes half-mast,
widen the smile – the obvious signals?
Where have you been hiding, hypocrite,
and so well, during conversation?
You could have warned me, made some sign,
and I'd have left earlier.
Or maybe you did, and I wouldn't believe it.
Overcome as with acne, against my intention,
with desire to challenge the neutral, indifferent –
a spreading rash that damaged a friendship.
She saw, he felt, the cheek proffered
too near to be merely cordial.
What did you do to me? I was so careful,
sure you were faithful. What other impulse
do you enclose that I thought mastered,
won over to reason?

It accosts you when you least expect it.
Like a crafty hustler or neglected cousin.
The urge to spin in someone else's orbit
that brings both legs too near each other.
It springs out at you in the safest places:
bus-stop, news-stand, lecture hall, taxis.
For it has a tiny pied-à-terre, desire,
a cell, on blood's main arteries and highways.
X-rays don't show it, nor a polished mirror
nor metal. You can glimpse its passage
in the reflection of answering eyes.

Nightlift

and no sound.
What, then, who, bids me thus
to creep into the kitchen in the dark,
barefoot, cautious?
The call of nature, as it's called, I've settled.
Now some less insistent force
leads me here to gaze across the road.
It's not yet five.
Three lights, three lives go on in shrouded buildings,
and in the convent hard by one goes out.
Time to sing the Maker. What Maker?
No Matter. No puzzling out the answer.
A call, triggered by those panes of light –
somebody is paying attention –
but springing from an undetected source.
Why that one out? A passing need, a nightmare
worsted, then back to unarmed sleep again?
Why are they up? Preparing for exams –
it's June – plotting cosines, or a coup,
writing wills out, making love? Perhaps
to sing their Maker. Before the dawn's
first sliver. When my father used to
sing Him. Never slept past five o'clock.
His urge to sing a simple, second
call of nature. To the giver of his breath
and all beginnings; who brought forth

both stars and dis-aster,
and after wind, earthquake, fire,
the still, small voice that followed.
Why ask my father if that voice still carried,
centuries later, above the cries
Elijah, unman-tled,
heard in the 'disinfecting' chamber?
Why ask that song before
sunrise be well-grounded?
Such questions not in keeping with this hour.

73

Night's lids, like mine, half-closed,
slowly open.
First stir of wings, a chirp, here and there,
and breath of beginnings.
There and here and thinly, by degrees,
darkness lifting.
The city's creatures weave their cobwebs, nests,
still, small-spoken.

It may well be, this hush, this spot
where I stand barefoot, looking out
behind now-opened lids,
a wellhead
I hadn't started out to find
but that I've travelled to all night.
Or maybe it's self-clarified:
three lights turned on and one snuffed out.
Who bids me thus? No answer.
No matter.

Drancy

What to do with this knowledge,
how to act?
The heart can just encompass one child's pain,
the mind imagine two, three graves
with rent compassion.
What organ of the body can contain
what 6 zeros after 6 convey?
Between the margins of this page
the truth won't fit.
'Imagine the hundred children to a room'
piled cheek upon soft cheek,
such great terror on such small limbs.
I read the facts that feed my rage.
Did they dream once, just for a minute?
Find respite in a dream one minute –
they had two days before the ovens –
did someone promise them raisins and almonds,
tell the story of a little goat?
Between the nightmares, did parents rock them
one last time, kiss them good-night?
What to do with this knowledge, how to act?
What Lachrymosa write about that Passion?
Weeping lasts but a week or so.
This happened two thousand weeks ago.
Turn to present misery
behind that window, about the globe . . .
But with such facts that feed such rage
the truth won't fit
between the margins of this page.

Notes from a Trip to Drancy

(taken with the painter R. B. Kitaj)

Looking at the Métro map, R.B. sees the name of Drancy. One can actually go there? It hadn't assumed an alias. 16 minutes out of Paris; used to be the stop before Auschwitz. Decide to see it. First absurdity: we could choose to go.

Meet at the Gare du Nord. Cold, clear day in March. Not sure of what we expect to see. Happened forty years ago. No quiver of response from man in ticket-booth. Buy round-trip' tickets. Second absurdity: we could come back.

Look through books and map on the train. Concerning the Jewish deportees:

'Generally, the deportees left Drancy from the station early in the morning. However, in October, 1942, the days getting shorter, the rounding up started the night before, because of the light, thus the deportees had to spend an extra night in those horrible wagons ... Those whose turn it was to leave were shoved into freight cars, sealed with lead before departure, not unsealed until they arrived at their destination. Only two pails of water in each wagon for the entire voyage. It would have to fill all their needs. Because of their number, the people could not sit ... The wagons being entirely closed, they could not see outside. A few small openings near the roof prevented these unfortunates from dying asphyxiated ... In only twelve months Drancy saw the deportation of 40,000 people ... Deportations on Sunday, Tuesday and Thursday, 3000 a week'. (*Drancy, 1941–1944*, Lycée Eugène Delacroix, Drancy, pp. 41, 64)

Arrive on time, this Saturday. Ask R.B.: 'So we arrive in Drancy. We look for a cab – a CAB? – then what do we say?' 'We say, "Take us to the concentration camp." '

DRANCY in big, clear letters. R.B. takes pictures. No warning in small letters to passengers to keep eye on hope, abandon. No Vergil for guide; only a suburb.

Commuting town. Workers, many from former colonies, Portugal, other foreigners. Communist mayor. Streets bear names of heroes, liberators: Bolivar, Juárez Auguste Blanqui; Sacco and Vanzetti – our American history meeting us.

No cab, town too small, start walking. Decide to find the town-hall for information. Ordinary houses, ordinary streets. R.B. takes pic-

76

tures of ordinariness, like an X-ray of an untroubled heart. Where's the murmur, no irregular beats, find the crack.

'Drancy is an internment center even before the first Jews arrive. In buildings begun before the war, and which were to become a garden city . . . the Germans pack in British, Yugoslav, Greek civilians temporarily. French prisoners follow, before being sent off to *Stalags* and *Oflags*'. (*op. cit.*, p. 11)

Town Hall the only distinguished-looking building so far. Bustling place: sections for drivers' licenses, marriage licenses, sports events. Woman in glasses and dark curly hair – too young to be of that generation – comes out to help us. Don't apologize for our request, neutral tone. 'We're Americans,' we say, drawing ourselves up like congressmen, 'and we'd like to see where it happened.' Woman looks sympathetic. We'd just missed an exhibition on 'what had happened'. First overt reference. A nerve touched. Lycéens of Drancy had collaborated on one of the books we were reading. Ask about the tunnel, dug in secrecy, the diggers themselves condemned but undertake the labor for others; an informer informed, secret betrayed, Germans astonished at feat, admire; deport. Where was it? She says it's now a Sports Center, would pass it on the way to the monument. Head for the monument – a stone tear, a concrete rip? Continue right.

Decide we'd have coffee before. Before what? What great job? Looking? Café crowded, smoky, Saturday morning lines for Lottery players. A few minutes, enough of postponing.

Two or three short blocks down, come to innocuous, adequate Sports Center. Some young people in front. Come to a block of flats, four stories high, U-shaped, holds 462 people. That was it. Where 7000 had been interned. Curtains in windows, figures moving, lawn in center.

'In the second half of August, 1942, 4000 children were brought to Drancy, without their parents . . . These children were from 2 to 12 years old. They were made to get down from the buses in the middle of the courtyard [now the lawn?] . . . The children got down and from then on the older ones [those over three years of age, of which there were about 1032] took the tiny ones by the hand and didn't let go throughout the short trip to the rooms. When they reached the stairs, the older ones took the small ones in their arms and, out of breath, carried them up to the fourth floor. There they remained near each other, hesitating a long time before sitting on the repugnantly filthy mattresses. The reunion there was of a tenderness

77

only unhappy children have the secret of . . . Try to imagine a dirty, stinking room, lit only by a blue night-light. Lying on the ground, the mattresses having lost their straw, filthy with excrement and stink of urine, 100 children to a room; imagine the shapes of girls and boys 2, 3, 4 years old, worn out with fatigue, sleeping one on top of the other, their soft, sweet, delicate cheeks pressed directly on the mattresses' filth . . . Or try to imagine the terrified, desperate looks of the tiniest ones who had to relieve themselves and couldn't do it alone, too small to go down the long, incommodious staircase to the toilets. These waited desperately for a woman to come along and help them, or another child.' (Georges Wellers, *L'Étoile jaune à l'heure de Vichy*, Paris, 1973, pp. 140, 141, 159)

From July to October, 1942, 5500 children thus exposed, in that housing project. Walk down to monument. Come to monument: steps on either side of center piece, flanked by two concave forms with words inscribed, in French, Yiddish, Hebrew. In French:

100,000 arrêtés, 1513 revenus, 1256 fusillés comme otages. Passant, recueille-toi et n'oublie pas [100,000 arrested, 1513 who came back, 1256 shot as hostages. You who pass by, think on this and do not forget].

A similar exhortation in Yiddish. Then, look closer. One line in Hebrew:

הַבִּיטוּ וּרְאוּ אִם־יֵשׁ מַכְאוֹב כְּמַכְאֹבִי

From Lamentations. Jeremiah in Drancy.

'Is it nothing to you, all ye that pass by? Behold and see if there be any sorrow like unto my sorrow, which is done unto me . . .' (Lamentations I:12, King James version); '. . . if there be any pain like my pain . . .' (*The Jerusalem Bible*).

SORROW! PAIN! 26 centuries ago. Copy inscription. Take pictures. Find bus back to station; at bus-stop a lycée crowd of boys and girls in their prime, adolescent equivocalities, pink cheeks. Get on train back to Gare du Nord.

Careful of what we say. Words are bold about other places, other horrors: plague, earthquake, famine, madmen. In Uganda, Chile, Siberia, Cambodia. But words walk away from Auschwitz and Treblinka; give up their swords and even ploughshares. Carry a permanent ulcer. There are degrees, even of evil.

Suspect literature. Remember the incinerated Jew is a beast of literature, by it created. A myth of usury, usury, usury. Even Goethe and Dostoevsky played with it. For readers' consumption.

78

The Uses of Poetry

For S.B. (13 April 1906–22 December 1989)

I

A Bible-reading man, he came and left
between two holy days he didn't much observe:
the Good Friday of his birth, near the Christmas of his death.
His life between, a pilgrim's progress with a smile
for what he saw along the way and wrote of,
oversleeping, age and hope and sloth.
Then saw, and wrote of, wrenched along the way,
age and hope and helpless weeping. But
he would have, reading those two states, rejected both
as most remotely holding but one part
or more than minute dose
of the inexpressible, whole truth
of how it is, it was.

II

He showed the shortest way to get across
a line like this:
crossed out such words as these to get to
speechlessness.
He crossed out rivers to get to their stones.
To get to the bottom, when the crisis is reached
and truth-telling begins.
Whatever he knew he knew to music.
He found the pace for misery,
matched distress to syncope, and joke
to a Beethoven stop at the punch line.
But thought that he'd failed to find failure's pulse.
What that says about failure,
music and us.

III

'You' is now 'he', an aftermath.
A nuance he'd appreciate.
He himself raised small auxiliaries
to their highest exponent,
like 'could' like a modest 'would'
from their wistful incertitude.
Not for him the mighty line of Marlowe
or verbal towers and plains of wrath.
It takes more lines, as though we could,
for us to follow, and if we would.
Who else could write a play about a single
inhaled, exhaled, breath?
What it says about us, reading
what those pilgrim's eyes had seen,
that we halt with recognition, yes, that's how
it was, it is, this life of mine.

IV

We'll feast no more with him at poetry's board
between puffs of his cigar.
Even in his coma he recited a stream
of Keats, Yeats, Hölderlin,
Apollinaire, Goethe and Verlaine,
Dante and Matthias Claudius
(for those who ask what one needs poetry for).
It wasn't their deeds made their poems sing in his head.
But he was what he wrote – should that make a difference
in the way we're warmed by printed fire – should
it matter, that his life had justified
his meter – give more credence
to the words about age and hope(lessness)
and suffering, earned, like daily bread?
That kindness was as easily picked up with him
as a fork at the table,
and pettiness as easily put aside?
That finding one so simply good
could make us as simply grateful –
what that says about goodness and us . . .

Towards the end, he gave everything away
not already given abroad;
everything transportable,
except friends' paintings and his old compass,
Samuel Johnson's Dictionary;
then waited in his small, bare room
for the scissors of Atropos.

V

His final act of tact was to leave a tomb
for friends to come and lean upon.
A slab with Samuel Beckett carved on it
for him whom everyone called Sam,
the full name only on books and documents.
There are plants, and scribbled notes;
one insisted – in despair? – 'Godot will come'.
As though to cast out doubt. What
it says of our position,
and such insistence,
that he may not.

Prepared his life for death his whole work through.
It wasn't morbid, or something we resented,
but inherent in a script
not memorized or taken for granted.
Like a soldier, staying at his post
with no relay in view,
holding out because one must.
Rast, du Krieger. Krieg ist aus.

You knew we'd grieve your passing, and also knew
we would go on.
Somehow we do.
Like Krapp and Hamm and Murphy. More and less.
You're at that part of the script where poets rest.
But how that leaves
the rest of us.